ALSO BY RAE ARMANTROUT:

Extremities, The Figures, 1978
The Invention of Hunger, Tuumba, 1979

PRECEDENCE

precedence

Some of these poems have appeared in Bluefish, Crawl Out Your Window, Credences, Feminist Studies, Hills, How(ever), Ironwood, O.ars, Partisan Review, This, Vanishing Cab, and The World.

This project is in part supported by a grant from the National Endowment for the Arts in Washington, D.C., a federal agency.

Library of Congress Cataloging in Publication Data

Armantrout, Rae, 1947—
   Precedence.

   I. Title.
PS3551.R455P7 1985   811'.54   84-22926
ISBN 0-930901-23-1
ISBN 0-930901-24-X (pbk.)

PRECEDENCE

Rae Armantrout

PRECEDENCE

PRECEDENCE

PRECEDENCE

PRECEDENCE

PRECEDENCE

PRECEDENCE

BURNING DECK
Providence

for Aaron

Contents

Double

So these are the hills of home. Hazy tiers
nearly subliminal. To see them is to see
double, hear bad puns delivered with a wink.
An untoward familiarity.

Rising from my sleep, the road is more
and less the road. Around that bend are pale
houses, pairs of junipers. Then to *look*
reveals no more.

Postcards

Man in
the eye clinic
rubbing his
eye—

too convincing. Like
memory.

My parents' neighbors' house,
backlit,
at the end of their street.

Single Most

Leaves fritter.

Teased edges.

It's vacillation that pleases.

Who answers for
the 'whole being?'

This is
only the firing

÷

Daffy runs across
the synapses, hooting
in mock terror.

Then he's shown
on an embankment, watching
the noisy impulse pass.

÷

But there's always a steady hum
shaped like a room
whose door must lead to
what really

where 'really'
is a nervous
tic as regular

÷

as as   as as

the corner repeats itself

÷

Dull frond:
giant lizard tongue
stuck out
in the murky distance
sight slides off
as a tiny elf.

÷

Patients are asked to picture
health as an unobstructed
hall or tube

through which Goofy now tumbles:
Dumb luck!

Unimagined
creature scans postcard.

÷

Conclusions can be drawn.

Shadows add depth
by falling

while deep secrets
are superseded—

quaint.

Exhaling
on second thought

Shut

Sanitainer. No one can doubt sunlight's bene-
ficence. A cozy press on the solar plexus.
The yard is fenced so I can have parties.
Prefer an unnamed ensemble. Magic, or the
image of attenuated fairies, was constantly
presented, though captioned unreal.

The smell of perfume reminds me of depart-
ment stores. A perfect fit may count as an
embrace. An arm of daisies naturally juts into
the lawn. Double meaning gets us off the dead
level. Wedgies are high heels pretending not
to be. The pink cloud and the purple one are
beautiful for having the same curlicue, while
two alyssums, drooping from the bouquet,
one above the other, take a pretty pose.

Elastic folk follow content in cartoons. Car
lots flirtatiously twinkle. Shaky intent creep-
ing toward the store: whatever that was
Mother once offered. Old-fashioned pumps
market a nod at ingenious constraint. On
the ledge behind our fences we play outlaw.
A babyish interest in minor characters could
disrupt the tale.

A web of 'issues' connects an imaginary citizenry. Chocolates are described as "home-fashioned." Tidy outfits to offset a growing slackness of feature. Who will argue things speak in the act of bursting? Gradually the street lapses into nightmare's non-embrace. At the crook a snarl pulses.

The lively resent unwary approaches. Emphasis is all. Aaron exclaims, "Truck in the tree." The jealous God expands to obliterate locale. Sunlight drums on closed eyelids. Weeds bristle.

"Paint?" "No!" "Trigger?" "No!" The mad detest familiar phantoms. Chief Gates plans to demonstrate controversial choke hold. Mother chose a blue box labeled "Commodore." Bumper cars jerk giddily on a tour of the replica. The uninvited will ring after symmetry clangs shut.

Traveling through the Yard

(from William Stafford)

It was lying near my back porch
in the gaudy light of morning—
a dove corpse, oddly featherless,
alive with flies.
I stopped,
dustpan in hand, and heard
them purr over their feast.
To leave that there would make some stink!
So thinking hard for all of us,
I scooped it up, heaved it
across the marriage counselor's fence.

Latter Day

1

When the particular
becomes romantic—

    blue bird,
        green nut,
            thin beak!

2

Porthole
in stucco,
bungalow—

like forgetting
what I meant.

3

In your absence, dear sir, this acquired
a wild salience.

4

A stillness as if
someone's finished speaking—

evening shadows
under carpet swirls.

*elaboration
of an idea
but forms
early it—
and agreement in
regard in
coming info
non judge
mentally*

Admission

The eye roves
back and forth, as
indictment catches up?

If shadows tattoo
the bare shelf,
they enter by comparison? *with plentitude?*

A child's turntable fastened
to the wall with a white cord
will not? *turn?*

Unless on its
metal core
an unspeakable radiance . . .

Think in order
to recall
what the striking thing

resembles.
(So impotently
loved the world

Compound

Flat
destroyers dawn
on haze
beyond Convair's low roof
and bare on-
ramps curling
up:
gray-white
congruence near to
the invisible.
While in this
car the round
drumbeats of "Mona"
fill our chests

metaphor

sky-scape

Compound two

Because
the child is,
silently,
far down
a diminished walk
I turn and call
the weather
"hot and
strange."
Uncovering
your teeth,
you glare

Through Walls

Stomach: lonely. *← thats where lonely lives*

Curled up in the
familiar ring
she went to sleep.

What a world, little churl!

Raw grass blades and
these spear-headed weeds,
dishevelled.

                Sun glancing.

Heat
did not
come home

to whom?

As if porous . . .
                Passing through

      ÷

Hungry for a garden's
whispered care.

Those blues and pinks.

                    Who has
saved some for you

may part
the afternoon from an evening
looked to, and
looking back
or down on our
walled-off suspense.

"There's more," we are
to understand.

Excreting one more
link, and putting
a leaf back
on either side, a fin, a stroke, this
slow progress.

                ÷

The awful thing
if every spurt
left him—

Anonymous Phrase—

in here   and there it
surfaces
under the hidden eyes of
Brer Fox and Brer Bear.

"Nana, na, nana."

÷

Ready tongue.

Coming back at
her sister, then
willing
to address the world's
intelligent and
uninhabited designs.

Most at home when
well-known
words come through
the metal
wires, the unseen
"transformers"

          saying
". . . reminds me of my home
far away."

Fiction *yes the world is*

Excitement of being someone else about whom a remark was imagined dominated her morning.

Being young, he drew weather and taped it on the walls.

Everywhere posed scenes solicited explanation.

The bumper-sticker on the white pick-up read, "Alien."

It was exhausting and provocative.

One might have admired a work composed of such obscure and equivocal elements for its durability.

But believing was eating, day by day, the long, extraneous fibers, and swallowing fast.

Swollen kindness and cruelty could be seen
from a great distance.

Children grew from our exaggerations.

The new television perched upon the console
of the old.

A ballerina fluttered on toe before a hammer
and sickle.

(What did the bitter, green nodules say to
the smeared glass?)

A Black man in a Union Jack t-shirt was
yelling, "Do you have any idea *what I mean?*"

pun Development is History

A short sidewalk
meanders
between boulevard and
parking—

some shrub
tucked
in every bend.

       Saw-toothed
foliage feints toward
an abstraction of grazing?

Does it matter what's fallen
at the perfect intervals—

so long as
we're on top of it,
I mean?

"Will the owner
  of the red Datsun
  in the Motor Home section
  of the B lot . . ."

Entries: look

1

something embarrassed and distracted,
rubbing up and down one side,
refusing to look or run a
hand thru hair like that's
hackneyed—so obviously
a statement it opens itself
to the accusation of untruth.

IS THAT YOU?

Afraid stopping would draw notice?
Ashamed to move purposely?

ARE YOU SICK OF ME?

2

Something has been left obscure, though
writing could decide the case.

Any instance is a fragment, might
be deceptive.

Only instances are seen.

Years pass:
Face to the tacit

3

Once
on top, always
move another's arms and
legs askew to show
'who's boss' or
signal the beginning of a
designated area, a little rough
so set apart.

DON'T LOOK AT ME LIKE THAT!

4

Caught, your eyes
take on expression
too quickly.

There's something to be parried
with a question or smile.

WHAT DO YOU WANT?

The arbitrary
message is broadcast
absence.

5

Not knowing
what to say to us
he waggles fingers,
feeble signals or mechanical twitches,
toward his small grandson.

WHAT DO YOU WANT?

What is recognition? A long look
that confirms your *Golden Gloves,*
St. Louis, crooner's
voice—those words
lit up?

The set blinks
on and on

LOOK HERE!

6

side by side
to laugh at the programs,
feeling a muted suspense
like something

"telling"

"a last long look"

"happens in the end"

Precedence

The dead boy
was found
clasping, "wrapped around"
a tree,
one chosen in a
roiling wilderness,
the urgent dream
where love gives way to rescue.
Or rescue to love.

chooses 2 ways
of saying it

Quotation

Where a class can be identified,
a goddess would appear.

Pointedly, such leaves
line up.

Matched and tattered.

Flipping the light on
(and on)

"As I must have said . . ."

Immortality's likeness—looking
from one to the next.

Another Tongue

"More experienced." Random twitches parted by a wind. Pretend this is a song about this. Drawn out emphasis of their "muy bien" not like our "very well." We relish the far villages—nestled and lost.

Under the lit suggestion of a forest canopy. Fashion lets us understand what a thing means. Warmer, more stylized, less sincere? The spectre of all stresses differently held. It is hard to say which shocks they will absorb, which guard themselves against.

Vaunted pockets. Children must list the attributes of (Col. Sander's) Kentucky. Coercion lets us understand what a thing means. Abstracted shapes of antique tools decorate the lobby. We're comfortable now with the exploratory process, if not with the stranger's mouth.

We plan to view that stream resembling thought. Partition, confusion, shading? What if they do not say "jungle" when maneuvering through high grass? A pregnant negative —the orchid nods and nods. Rushed twitches present themselves as the 'heart' of matter.

We live for the differences among related parts. This time the little singer stops before delivering the word "Aint." A pause invites us to picture. In the distance—numb flutter. Hover flies mix up.

Sigh

Homesick for
acquiescence:

Mother and child in
an old

car's leaden
exhalation.

Memories of waiting
to open the

present
wreathe our prospect of

future time

in a weird
holiday cheer.

Blocks

Early learning brackets
the notorious product—

a long, brown string of
vinyl booths—

in the correct light.

A screen's blue
nest of dots,
thrashing,

renders simple
blocks of time.

Secretly

1
Pending

point of *entry*.

(Prestige surrounding 'entry'
bullies passers-by

as melody line
obscures dry fields. *Discrete*
bushes

2
What's highlighted?

"Leukemia Boy
dies."

Voice of outraged
normalcy
being one item.

One
character.

Lincoln was a quiet
melancholy.

A trademark-like
stuttering.

Chevron
takes the form

of a meek,
purple

dinosaur.

3

He thinks *light* and *monstrous,*
motherless, traffic, exposed

if not with relish, then
furtive pride.

Real 'diamonds'—
a precious code.

This is a private room,
a contraction,
a phrase truncated
like the hidden name of God—

standing in for everything.
Obscene.
This is a sick room.

4

Until I see a beauty
in disinterest, in digression! Juggling
vs. cathexis.

Then there is the juggler
as idol of romance.

(Wry concession
being one item

with the august role
of 'Wildness'
in the scheduled pageant.

The point being
one term
has been crowned
secretly.

Round

Do the children want a face
drawn on everything?

Delighted to be shown
cat's eyes
among painted leaves.

Smiling
neon star:
beacon

round which empty,
mauve evening.

Home Federal

A merchant is
probing for us
with his chintz curtain
                effect.

     ÷

"Ha, ha, you missed me,"
a dead person says.

     ÷

There's the bank's
Colonial balcony
where no one has
                ever stood.

Atmospheric

Let up one half note above horizon line, a
steel-edged, sad and glinting containment, or
sexily exploded sunset smear—mystic because
absolutely fixed: an artful backward glance
which has assumed unearthly proportions.
Indeed he is happiest when his family is
scattered in the atmosphere, silenced, yet in-
flecting all with the memory of speech.

The Music

Great preponderance waddles. Naked
buzz composed of what?

If background noise becomes clear speech?
Half-sensical, mocking: a parent's voice
we won't be able to discount.

I want to leave someplace out!

To know the world must mean to know how
to get through .

On every bar the music shifts.
"I can't seem to get comfortable."

This book was designed and printed on Warren Olde Style by Rosmarie Waldrop. The cover by Keith Waldrop uses a photograph by the author. The text was linotyped in 12 pt. Palatino by Mollohan Typesetting in West Warwick, R.I. Smyth-sewn by New Hampshire Bindery in Concord. There are 1000 copies, of which 50 are cloth-bound and signed.